Corrupt Bargain!

"They Stole the Election!"

Harlow Giles Unger

New York Times Best-Selling Author

Table of

Contents

Illustrations

About the Author

Harlow Giles Unger is a veteran journalist, broadcaster, educator, and historian. The author of more than 30 books, he is a former Distinguished Visiting Fellow in American History at George Washington's Mount Vernon. The *Washington Post* named him one of America's premier presidential biographers for his best-selling biography of James Monroe--*The Last Founding Father.* He is a graduate of Yale University.

Also by Harlow Giles Unger

John Quincy Adams
The Last Founding Father
Lion of Liberty (Patrick Henry)
The Genêt Affair
The Last Man To Die in the American Revolution
The Jefferson Conspiracy (Some Called It Treason)
George Washington's Magick Money Man

Chapter 1

Mr. Clay Will Call

Only 35 years after America's Founding Fathers conceived the world's first experiment in popular rule, a terrifying headline leaped off newspaper front pages across the nation:

AN END TO LIBERTY!

The story began innocently enough—an ordinary note had been left in the John Quincy Adams reception hall, announcing the writer's intent to visit later that day. Adams smiled when he saw the sender's name. What he could not see or smell was the poisoned ink on the note— poison so powerful it would change the course of his life and that of the nation. All America—and the world—would soon learn the contents of that note—and more.

Only a while earlier, Adams seemed on his way to the presidency of the United States. As Secretary of State, he held the same office that had catapulted three previous Americans to the presidency. Thomas Jefferson, James Madison, and the current president, James Monroe had all been secretaries of state before stepping into the nation's highest office. John Quincy Adams fully intended doing the same. He had been the best secretary of state by far and was the most qualified candidate vying for the nation's highest office.

And that had not been by chance. From the moment he was born, his parents—soon-to-be President John Adams and his wife Abigail--had groomed John Quincy for the presidency. Indeed, Adams had taken his son Quincy—only 12 at the time--on diplomatic missions to Europe, before sending him to Harvard University to study law. As a young man, Quincy—his intimates all called him Quincy--as a young man Quincy had served under President Washington, lived with and got to know Ben Franklin. Quincy lunched with Lafayette, Jefferson, Wellington, and Dickens, took long morning walks with Russia's czar, and held discussions with Britain's king. He had been American minister to six European countries and helped negotiate the peace that ended the War of 1812. As President James Monroe's secretary of state—his current position--he engineered the seizure and annexation of Florida and written the core provisions of the Monroe Doctrine ending foreign colonization in the Americas.

There was no question he was the most qualified and best trained candidate to succeed James Monroe as President in 1824—especially since his friends all agreed with him that his chief opponent was little more than "a barbarian who could hardly spell his own name."

So when Quincy opened the note announcing the imminent visit of a caller that afternoon, he fully expected the caller to stop by with a key to the White House:

> *Mr. Clay's compliments to Mr. Adams, and if he be not engaged, Mr. C. will call this evening at six O'clock to see him on an affair of business.*"[1]

The note provoked a rare grin on John Quincy Adams's stern face. He assumed that "Mr. Clay"—Speaker-of-the-House Henry Clay of Kentucky--was coming to announce his—Clay's—withdrawal from the 1824 presidential race. Adams fully expected the Speaker would then pledge him his votes and lift him to the highest seat of power in the nation.

1.   John Quincy Adams

Speaker Clay, along with Adams, Secretary of the Treasury William H. Crawford, of Georgia, and the man Adams called "the barbarian" had all been candidates for president in 1824, until a serious illness forced Secretary Crawford to withdraw his name from consideration. That left only three candidates. Adams, Speaker Clay, and "the barbarian."

Clay, however, was no longer as popular as he had once been. He had devoted his life to public service and, by the time he became House Speaker, he was unquestionably America's greatest statesman. He had served on the peace commission that ended the War of 1812 with Britain and reached the heights of statesmanship as author of the historic Missouri Compromise that prevented civil war in America.

The Missouri territory had applied for statehood five years earlier in 1919, but a majority of Missouri's settlers were slaveholders, and admission to the Union would have given slave states a voting advantage in the U.S. Senate over non-slave states and ensured survival of slavery in the United States in perpetuity. New York's abolitionist Representative James Tallmadge, Jr., however, demanded that Missouri be admitted as a free state, giving free states the majority in both

House and Senate and the votes to emancipate slaves in the entire nation.

True to the state's traditional epithet—"stubborn as a Missouri mule"—Missouri's abolitionists and slaveholders debated for months, with each group refusing to yield and warning the opposition: "If you persist, the Union will be dissolved!"

Clay stepped in, however, with a brilliant compromise for what threatened to become a bitter—even bloody--conflict. By allowing Maine to separate from Massachusetts and join the Union as a free-soil state and letting Missouri join as a slave state, the Missouri Compromise would not disrupt the 50-50 division of the states, thus keeping the union in peace and intact.

Although Clay postponed the danger of civil war, only a minority of Americans considered him a hero. The vast majority cared less about saving the Union than they did about either retaining slavery, if they were southerners, or abolishing it, if they were northerners. Both sides believed only bullets and bloodshed would resolve the issue. Both sides saw Clay's compromise as a cowardly postponement and voted for "anyone but Clay" in the presidential election of 1824.

Of nearly 353,000 votes cast, Clay won only about 47,500, or 13 percent of the popular vote, and 37 of the 270 Electoral College votes.

Astute politician that he was, though, Henry Clay refused to let the impact of the Missouri Compromise dampen his presidential ambitions. Instead, he took the next best step: to seek appointment as Secretary of State—a post that had been the traditional, all-but certain stepping stone to the Presidency. Former presidents Jefferson,

Madison, and Monroe had all been secretaries of

state before moving into the nation's highest office.

With that in mind, Speaker of the House Henry

Clay of Kentucky sent the note saying he intended

visiting the current secretary of state and

presidential candidate John Quincy Adams. As

Adams had done when he received Clay's note,

Clay now smiled as he read Adams's reply:

*Mr. Adams, with his respectful compliments to Mr.
Clay, will be happy to see him this evening at 6
O'clock. Sunday 9, Jany 1825*
\

At 6 p.m. on "Sunday 9, Jany 1825,"

Speaker Henry Clay arrived at the Washington,

D.C., house on F Street, where John Quincy Adams

lived with his family. Adams's scholarly mind

produced this detailed account of the meeting after

Clay had left.

2. Henry Clay

"Mr. Clay came at six and spent the evening with me in a long conversation explanatory of the past and prospective of the future. He said that the time was drawing near when the choice must be made in the House of Representatives of a President from the three candidates presented by the electoral colleges; that he had been much urged and solicited with regard to the part in that transaction that he should take and had not been five minutes landed at his lodgings before he had been applied to by a friend of Mr. Crawford's in a manner so gross that it had disgusted him; that some of my friends also, disclaiming, indeed, to have any authority from me [Adams], had repeatedly appealed to him, directly or indirectly, urging considerations personal to himself as motives to his cause. He had thought it

best to reserve his determination to
himself, first, to give a decent time for his
own funeral solemnities as a candidate
and, secondly, to prepare and predispose
all his friends to a state of neutrality
between the three candidates who would
be before the House, so that they might be
free ultimately to take that course which
might be most conducive to the public
interest. He wished me, as far as I might
think proper, to satisfy him with regard to
some principles of great public importance,
but without any personal considerations for
himself. In the question to come before the
House between General Jackson, Mr.
Crawford, and myself, he had no hesitation
in saying that his preference would be for
me."

According to Adams, Clay

said that with the House of

Representatives preparing to choose

the next President, he, as House

Speaker, had been "much urged and

solicited with regard to the part in

that transaction that he [Clay] should

take…

"The time had now come in which he might be explicit in his communication with me, and he had for that purpose asked this confidential interview. He wished me as far as he might think proper to satisfy him with regard to some principles of great public importance, but without any personal considerations for himself. In the question to come before the House between General Jackson…and myself, he had no hesitation in saying that his preference would be for me."[2]

In effect, the two men agreed to undermine American democracy to prevent the American people from electing a president who, the two men believed, would undermine American democracy. There was little question in either man's mind that they would be defying the will of the people, but by ensuring the election of John Quincy Adams as the next President of the United States, they would prevent the man they called a "barbarian" from seizing power.

3.Andrew Jackson

Far from being a barbarian, however, Andrew Jackson was in reality a prominent Tennessee lawyer and a former judge who had served in both the U.S. Senate and the House of Representatives. He had also been one of America's most successful and enormously popular military leaders. He had fought in the Revolutionary War, been captured by the British. Then, when a sadistic British officer demanded that Jackson polish his boots, Jackson refused, only to have the British officer drew his sword and slash Jackson's face. It left a scar that would earn the awe and admiration

of Americans for the rest of Jackson's life.

In 1812, Jackson raised a militia that pushed

the British out of Pensacola, Florida. He then led his

men to Louisiana, where, on January 8, 1815, he

defeated a powerful British army in a fierce battle

that cost the British 2,500 men and forced them to

withdraw from America forever.

News of Jackson's incredible victory sent

American spirits soaring and raised Jackson to the

heights of heroic adulation for avenging the British

capture of the nation's capital in Washington and

their 1814 burning of the U.S. Capitol and White

House.

In 1817, General Jackson returned to the

military to lead an invasion of Spanish-held Florida

and obtain eventual U.S. acquisition of that territory

from Spain. Again, he won a hero's acclaim across

America, and, in 1822, the Tennessee legislature voted to send him to the U.S. Senate and nominate him for U.S. president.

Six feet, one inch tall, straight and strong as a hickory tree—his nick-name was "Old Hickory—he drew admirers to his side wherever he went. A planter and hunter himself, he talked and mingled freely, joyfully with all comers. He used the common man's language, told tall tales, and regaled ordinary folks wherever he went. Mobs inevitably gathered around him, followed him wherever he went—cheering, shouting, and drinking as they went until they fell down drunk. In effect, they repelled the staid Harvard graduate John Quincy Adams, who called Jackson a "barbarian" for embracing them.

In the election that followed, the entry of four candidates so divided the Electoral College votes that none could capture the majority required

for election. To the outrage of many—even most--

Americans, Jackson had won a crushing majority of

popular votes--38,149 more than Adams. 151, 271

<u>Voting in the 1824 Election:</u>
<u>Popular Votes   Elect. College</u>

	Popular Votes	Elect. College
Jackson	151,271	99
Adams	113,122	84
Crawford	47,531	41
Clay	40,856	37

votes to Adams's 113,122, and the most, if not the

majority, of Electoral College votes—99 to John

Quincy's 84.

<u>But</u> too many of his votes came in states

with too few votes in the Electoral College, thus

denying the will of the electorate. Most Americans

didn't even know what the Electoral College was,

where it was, or who was in it. They certainly

hadn't purposely voted for anyone in it and were furious that an anonymous band of so-called "electors" could steal the election away from the people. Many called for its destruction, but no one seemed to know where it was or how to find it. Critics raged at the undemocratic way it chose the president, arguing it must have been open to manipulation by charlatans.

The question of how to select the best presidential candidates, however, had plunged the Constitutional Convention into near-chaos for weeks in the summer of 1787. Almost every delegate offered some plan with flaws that always offset its advantages. Virginia planter George Mason raged that foreign interests would benefit from "the corruptibility of the men chosen."

Chaired by George Washington, the Convention convened in mid-May 1787, with

Virginia Governor Edmund Randolph proposing

that "a National Executive be…chosen by the

National Legislature [i.e., Congress]" Contrary

arguments immediately plunged the Convention

into chaos. Making matters worse, delegates had

sealed the windows of the Pennsylvania State

House (now Independence Hall) to keep

proceedings secret, and Philadelphia's blistering

summer heat turned the site into an oven that sent

tempers rising with the temperature.

Philadelphia's Gouverneur Morris countered

Randoph's proposal, demanding

that U.S. citizens elect the President. "If the people

should elect, they will… prefer some man of

distinguished character…of continental reputation.

If the Legislature elects, it will be the work of

intrigue, of cabal, and of faction. It will be like the

election of the pope by a conclave of cardinals; real merit will rarely be the title to the appointment."

The aging Benjamin Franklin agreed that failure to permit the people to choose the chief magistrate was "contrary to republican principles. In free governments, the rulers are the servants, and the people their superiors and sovereigns."

Made up largely of America's wealthiest men, the Convention rejected Franklin's suggestion. Connecticut's Roger Sherman claimed the country was too large for a popular vote: "The people will never be sufficiently informed." South Carolina planter Charles Pinckney agreed, warning that the three most populous states (Virginia, Pennsylvania, and Massachusetts at the time) would combine to elect the president and thwart the will of all other states. Nine states agreed and voted down popular elections.

Chaos ensued, with delegates out-shouting one another until General Washington—all 6 feet 2 inches of him--rose above them all and demanded order!

Virginia Governor Randolph tried explaining that all proposals under consideration posed "the danger of monarchy" and "civil war." The executive "will be in possession of the sword: Make him too weak, the legislature will usurp his powers. Make him too strong, he will usurp those of the legislature…..a civil war will ensue, and the commander of the victorious army will be the despot of America."

As the debate intensified, Washington again barked for order and warned delegates to settle their differences: "There are seeds of discontent in every part of the union ready to produce disorders, if…the present Convention should not be able to devise…a more vigorous and energetic government," he cautioned.

On August 31, most delegates admitted defeat and turned the problem over to a committee of eleven—one member from each participating state--to produce a binding resolution. With six slave-state delegates in the majority, the committee gave each state government power to appoint, directly or by popular vote, "a number of electors equal to the whole number of senators and representatives to which the state may be entitled in Congress." Those electors would choose the President and Vice President.

Delegates from the North were furious. Non-voting slaves would inflate the population that determined the number of each southern state's representatives in Congress, allowing, a relatively small number of southern freeholders—the wealthy white plantation and property owners who owned most of the land and slaves in the South—to elect a disproportionately large number of electors.

"The [geographically] large states have a very undue influence in the appointment of the president," Luther Martin, a Maryland lawyer, argued. "There is no case where the states will have an equal voice…." Combined with his command over the armed forces, "these circumstances will enable him [a minority President], when he pleases, to become a king in name, as well as in substance, and establish himself in office not only for his own life but…to have that authority perpetuated to his family."[3]

The northern delegates, however, recognized that rejection of southern demands would end chances for a ratification of a constitution and formation of a union. Virginia alone was America's largest, most populous, wealthiest state—the essential core of any union. On September 12, 1787, therefore, the Electoral College was born.

The Constitutional Convention left each state free to decide how it would select its electors and whether or not electors would have to cast ballots according to voter preferences. No federal law prevented electors from disregarding preferences of those who appointed or elected them, allowing almost anyone to disregard the voting public and steal the election. In effect, the Founding Fathers had opened the way for a corrupt bargain to determine the president of the United States.

Chapter 2

The Electors

In the more than two centuries since the Constitution took effect, the Electoral College has elected five presidents who failed to win a majority of popular votes, and 214 "faithless electors" have disregarded voter preferences in 19 of 58 presidential elections. No "faithless electors" have ever been prosecuted.

Although Benjamin Franklin signed the Constitution, he was not enthusiastic: "I confess that I do not entirely approve this Constitution at present, but I am not sure I shall ever approve it." Washington agreed, conceding imperfections, but citing Article V permitting future amendments to remedy defects.

Washington, however, lived in a nation of 4 million people and 13 states--and fewer than 50,000 eligible voters--all white, male property owners. He did not--and could not--envision his nation exploding into an empire stretching from the Atlantic Ocean across one-fourth of the planet's circumference, midway into the Pacific Ocean.

In 1787, when he chaired the Constitutional Convention, he did not—and could not—even envision the nation of 1824, with nearly 10 million people in 24 states, each with conflicting and often irreconcilable interests. The inevitable result was the failure of both Andrew Jackson and John Quincy Adams to win a majority of Electoral College votes needed to claim the presidency.

Although Americans embraced Jackson as a national hero and made him the overwhelming favorite in the months leading up to the 1824 election, and although he ran away with the popular vote, the Electoral College determined that none of the four candidates had won election to the presidency. The Constitution now determined that the selection of the next President would be left to the House of Representatives, where each state would cast a single vote for its favorite candidate. Kentucky representative Henry Clay was Speaker. Besides his gavel, he wielded considerable influence over other members of the House. Before the House convened to vote on February 9, 1825. Clay's Kentucky delegation announced it would cast its vote for Adams, despite Jackson's overwhelming popular victory in Kentucky's election. Missouri and Ohio—two states Clay had won—followed suit, giving Adams the exact number of states—thirteen—that he needed to win the presidency. Jackson won seven, and Crawford four. **Congress then shocked the nation and the world by declaring Secretary of State John Quincy Adams the sixth President of the United States despite his paltry showing in the popular election.**

The public galleries in the house erupted into so frightening an uproar of booing and hissing that Speaker Clay ordered them cleared.

Three days later, the new president nominated Henry Clay as his secretary of state. In their minds—and the minds of their supporters--the two were the most qualified and perhaps the most brilliant men in United States history to hold their respective posts. Even their opponents could not dispute their qualifications. In addition, the two men—one from Massachusetts, the other from Kentucky--together with Vice President John C. Calhoun of South Carolina. represented the first presidential team to represent the entire country—

East, West, South, and North.

John Quincy Adams and Henry Clay were

certain their government would be the most perfect

in American history.

They were dead wrong!

CORRUPT BARGAIN! screamed the

headlines in several newspapers after the vote in

Congress put Quincy Adams in the White House.

SHAME! Ran another.

A third featured the most provocative of all,

citing Jackson himself and his tens of thousands of

supporters: **"THEY STOLE THE ELECTION!"**

Jackson and his followers were furious—

and rightfully so. After all, he had won by far the

largest share of popular votes with 42 percent as

well as the most Electoral College votes. Jackson

immediately declared that he would run in 1828

and, if elected, propose eliminating the Electoral College and replace it with direct elections by the people.

"I weep for the liberty of my country," Jackson sighed. "The rights of the people have been bartered for promises of office.... The voice of the people of the West have been disregarded, and demagogues barter them as sheep in the shambles for their own views and personal aggrandizement."[4]

Few members of the Washington political scene disagreed or doubted that John Quincy had promised, tacitly or otherwise, to reward Clay for his support. Knowing how Clay lusted for the presidency, all assumed that John Quincy would appoint him secretary of state, a stepping stone to the presidency for more than two decades. Rumors of "bargain & sale" swept across the political landscape, with some Jackson supporters growling about possible civil war and secession in the West.

The mood in the White House turned less than relaxed a few days after the House vote, when President Monroe hosted a reception for the President-elect. Indeed, the President was chatting with a guest when Andrew Jackson, still recovering from a debilitating illness, thrust his grim, gaunt face in the doorway. Armed as always with two pistols, he snapped his head from side to side until he spotted John Quincy. As the President and other celebrants held their collective breaths, Jackson bounded forward, broke into a warm smile, and, hand outstretched, offered John Quincy his congratulations.

Five days after his election victory, John Quincy announced his appointment of Henry Clay as secretary of state.

"So you see," Andrew Jackson wailed in outrage, "the Judas of the West has closed the contract and will receive thirty pieces of silver. His end will be the same. Was there ever witnessed such a bare-faced corruption in any country before?"

Others agreed that John Quincy and Clay had arranged a "corrupt bargain" that undermined the election process and deprived voters of their chosen candidate. New York Senator Martin Van Buren, who had backed Crawford's candidacy, was as outraged as Jackson, warning a Kentucky congressman that, in voting for Adams, "you sign Mr. Clay's political death warrant."[5]

Corrupt or not, in appointing Henry Clay secretary of state, John Quincy had also signed his own political death warrant as President. On March 4, 1829, Andrew Jackson was inaugurated as seventh President of the United

States. Ignoring tradition, John Quincy refused to attend the inauguration or attend the new President's White House reception afterwards. "I can yet scarcely realize my situation," he shuddered in disbelief, saying that "posterity will scarcely believe...the combination of parties and of public men against my character and reputation such as I believe never before was exhibited against any man since this Union existed."

Like Henry Clay, John Quincy Adams seemed oblivious to the outrage he and Clay had committed against the voting public of the United States and to the spirit of the Constitution in making the corrupt bargain that had allowed him into The White House. Ignoring the huige popular majority that Andrew Jackson commanded, Adams insisted that "the combination against me has been formed and is now exulting in triumph over me, for the devotion of my life and of all the faculties of my

soul to the Union and to the improvement, physical,

moral and intellectual, of my country.

"The North," he continued, "assails me for

my fidelity to the Union; the South, for my ardent

aspirations of improvement. Yet...passion,

prejudice, envy, and jealousy will pass. The cause

of Union and of improvement will remain, and I

have duties to it and to my country yet to

discharge."[6]

Although the vast majority of American

voters had rejected John Quincy and his vision for

America, he refused to accept their judgment and

vowed to continue his struggle to lead them and the

nation down what he envisioned as national his path

to greatness. His only uncertainty now was how to

do it.

Chapter 3

A New Beginning

After his 1828 defeat, President John Quincy Adams prepared to return to his father's house in Quincy, Massachusetts, resigned to a life of semi-retirement, puttering about the farm a bit, but focused on writing a biography of his father and practicing law part-time. His articles on international affairs found their way into scholarly journals, but as the summer progressedJohn Quincy became depressed. His only pleasures were walking and swimming, reading the Bible and Cicero's *Orations*, planting fruit trees and tending a garden of peas, beans, corn and other vegetables. He made half-hearted attempts at organizing his father's papers, rummaging through boxes and finding some mementoes of his youth–largely books, such as a fondly remembered edition of *Arabian Nights*.

"The more there was in them of invention, the more pleasing they were," he recalled. "My imagination pictured them all as realities, and I dreamed of enchantments as if there was a world in which they existed."[7] As ill-disposed as he was to public functions, he agreed to attend the bicentennial celebration of the founding of Boston on September 17, and, to his surprise, two honorary marshals escorted him from the State House to the Old South Church. Well-wishers hailed him as he passed, and even former Federalist adversaries approached with warm salutations.

At the end of the day, he attended a reception at the lieutenant governor's residence, where his friends and the editor of the Boston *Patriot* were huddling with Quincy Congressman

Reverend Joseph Richardson. After greeting the former President, they asked if they could visit him the following day. He agreed and, at the appointed time, they informed him that Richardson's parishioners had pleaded with him to retire from Congress to devote full time to his church, and he had agreed. They then asked him to run for Richardson's seat, assuring him that he would win without opposition and flattering him with the notion of "ennobling" the House of Representatives by the presence of a former President.

Always in character, John Quincy feigned disinterest, saying he would do nothing to support his candidacy. Explaining his familiar position on political campaigns, he asserted that if the people called on him of their own volition, he "might deem it my duty to serve.... I want the people to act spontaneously."[8] He made it clear, however, that he would remain independent of party affiliations and represent the whole nation, with his only political loyalty tied to national independence of all foreign ties and preservation of the Union.

His wife and Louisa and son Charles Francis were appalled that John Quincy would even consider returning to politics after the humiliation he had suffered. Louisa threatened not to accompany him if he returned to Washington–to no avail. The town of Quincy ignored his corrupt bargain with Henry Clay and voted overwhelmingly to return their former President to Washington, giving him 1,817 votes, while the two other candidates garnered a combined total of only 552 votes

"I am a member-elect of the Twenty-Second Congress," he wrote in joyful disbelief that night, and nothing Louisa could say could detract from his satisfaction. "My return to public life...is

disagreeable to my family," he admitted, "yet I can

not withhold my grateful acknowledgment to the

Disposer of human events and to the people of my

native region for this unexpected testimonial of

their continued confidence....

It seemed as if I was deserted by all mankind... In

the French opera of Richard Coeur-de-Lion, the

minstrel Blondel sings under the walls of his prison

a song, beginning:

> *O, Richard! O, mon Roi!*
> *L'univers t'abandonne.*[*]

"When I first heard this song, forty-five

years ago," John Quincy Adams ruminated, "it

---

[*] *O, Richard, my king. The world abandons*

thee.

made an indelible impression upon my memory, without imagining that I should ever feel its force so much closer to home. But this call upon me by the people of the district in which I reside, to represent them in Congress, has been spontaneous.... My election as President of the United States was not half so gratifying to my inmost soul. No election or appointment conferred upon me ever gave me so much pleasure.[9]

As his spirits revived, he finally coaxed Louisa into returning to Washington, and the two left in December. Along the way, he showed himself still a champion of public improvements by being among the first to ride on the new steam-driven train between Baltimore and Washington. And to his delight and Louisa's amazement, a crowd awaited to greet their return. Although he would not take his seat until 1832, three hundred callers came to their house on New Years Day, 1831, buoying his spirits still more and spurring him to seek out and meet members of Congress to determine their political views.

He attended the House of Representatives to learn the rules and study member quirks and tics, and, as he soaked up the thinking of his future colleagues, the joy of his return to politics spurred a renewed interest in scholarly pursuits, including poetry. By spring, when the time came to return to Quincy, he had re-read *Childe Harold, Don Juan,* and other works of Byron--and written his own epic, two-thousand line poem *Dermot MacMorrogh,* on Henry II's conquest of Ireland. He considered it his finest work and at least one publisher agreed, producing three successive editions.[*] On the way north, he stopped to see former President James Monroe, who was gravely ill in New York and destitute, living off the charity of his daughter and son-in-law at their New York City home.

After his return to Quincy, town officials invited him to give the July 4 oration, and he set to work on a fierce attack on the doctrine of "nullification," which had regained currency in the South in response to high federal tariffs on cotton goods. Thomas Jefferson had fathered the concept in 1798, when he was vice president and opposed the Alien and Sedition Acts of President John Adams.

---

[*] *Dermot MacMorrogh, or the Conquest of Ireland: and Historical Tale of the Twelfth Century,* in Four Cantos (Boston: Carter Hendee and Company, 1st ed., 1832; 2nd ed., 1832; 3rd ed., I. N. Whiting and Company, Columbus, Ohio, 1834).

Declaring the Constitution only "a compact" among sovereign states, Jefferson insisted that the states retained authority to restrain federal government actions that exceeded its constitutional mandate. Jefferson convinced the Kentucky legislature to approve a resolution allowing it to declare unconstitutional any federal government exercise of powers not specifically delegated by the Constitution. His protégé James Madison marched in lockstep and convinced the Virginia legislature "to interpose" its authority to prevent federal-government "exercise of...powers" not granted by the Constitution.[10]

Federalist legislatures in other states, however, declared the Virginia and Kentucky Resolutions "mad and rebellious" and rejected them by declaring U.S. courts to be the sole judges of constitutionality.

Vice president John Calhoun subsequently revived southern interest in the concept with an essay he called *South Carolina Exposition and Protest*. In it, he insisted that the tenth amendment gave every state the right to nullify a federal act if it deemed it a violation of the Constitution.

In his July 4 oration in Quincy, John Quincy countered by labeling the concept of state sovereignty an "hallucination" and nothing "less than treason"–a fierce charge that resounded across the country after an enterprising printer distributed more than 4,000 copies of his speech nationwide.

As John Quincy delivered his oration, James Monroe, the President he had served for eight years, died in New York–joining John Adams and Thomas Jefferson as the third of the first five presidents to die on July 4.

Asked to deliver a eulogy of Monroe at

Boston's Old South Church, John Quincy produced

a stirring reminder of Monroe's courage as an

officer during the Revolution, "weltering in his

blood on the field of Trenton for the cause of his

country."

Then John Quincy turned to his own–and

Monroe's--favorite subject: public improvements.

He urged mourners to "look at the map of United

North America, as it was...in 1783. Compare it with

the map of that same Empire as it is now...the

change, more than of any other man, living or dead,

was the work of James Monroe." John Quincy

recalled how Monroe had scoffed at Congress for

denying it had "the power of appropriating money

for the construction of a canal to connect the waters

of Chesapeake Bay with the Ohio."[11] He portrayed

the "unspeakable blessings" of Monroe's vision of a transnational network of roads and canals:

"Sink down, ye mountains!" John Quincy called out. "And ye valleys–rise!... Exult and shout for joy! Rejoice! that...there are neither Rocky Mountains nor oases of the desert, from the rivers of the Southern [Pacific] Ocean to the shores of the Atlantic Sea; Rejoice: that...the waters of the Columbia mingle in union with the streams of the Delaware, the Lakes of the St. Lawrence with the floods of the Mississippi; Rejoice! that...the distant have been drawn near...that the North American continent swarms with...hearts beating as if from one bosom, of voices speaking with but one tongue, of freemen constituting one confederated and united republic of brethren, never to rise...in hostile arms...to fulfill the blessed prophecy of ancient times, that war shall be no more.[12].

By the time he and Louisa began their return to Washington for the opening of Congress in December 1831, his eloquence had resounded across the nation, with both his July 4 oration and eulogy to Monroe having been published in most American newspapers. His corrupt bargain with Henry Clay all but forgotten, he found old political friends waiting to greet him everywhere he went.

In Philadelphia, Albert Gallatin, his associate in the Ghent treaty negotions that ended the War of 1812, asked him to preside at the Literary Convention then in session and won his appointment to a committee drawing up plans for a National Library and Scientific Institution.

By the time he reached Washington, his political enemies in Congress feared he was mounting a surreptitious campaign to recapture the presidency, and, to prevent that possibility, they shunted him into the least important committees. Instead of the committee on foreign affairs–"the line of occupation in which all my life has been passed"-- he found himself chairman of the committee of manufactures, "for which I feel myself not to be well qualified. I know not even enough of it to form an estimate of its difficulties."[13]

Although any member of the House could introduce a bill relating to anything he chose, by tradition, members limited the bills they proposed to matters within the purview of their own committees. To escape what he considered a procedural strait-jacket, he decided to flaunt House tradition and use the right of every committee chairman to read citizen petitions on the House floor–regardless of their content.

On his first day in Congress, therefore, he hurled his first thunderbolt on the floor of the House, shocking both sides of the aisle with not one, but *fifteen* petitions from Pennsylvania Quakers, "praying for the abolition of slavery and the slave trade in the District of Columbia.." By rules adopted by the First Congress in 1790, the House had agreed to remain silent on the question of abolition–largely because of South Carolina's threat to walk out at the mention of abolition or slavery. The Capitol all but imploded as echoes of John Quincy Adams's voice filled the air with the long-forbidden words.

"I was not more than five minutes on my feet but I was listened to with great attention," John

Quincy smiled, "and when I sat down, it seemed to myself as if I had performed an achievement."[14]

He had indeed performed an achievement. Although most of the House rose as one to roar its disapproval, the former President had burst open the doors of Congress to abolitionist voices for the first time in decades–voices that other congressmen had routinely ignored for forty years and would never be able to ignore again. Although Pennsylvania Quakers were not his constituents, he had proclaimed himself a representative of the whole nation, and the whole nation now took him at his word, inundating him with petitions they knew their own representatives would never accept.

It was not a good time to be a proponent of abolition in America, however. Only months before, a black preacher, Nat Turner, had led an insurrection in Virginia, killing 57 white people, including eighteen women and twenty-four children. Only swift retaliation by U.S. Marines prevented the insurrection from spreading into North Carolina. Although 100 blacks had been killed and 20 later executed, the specter of future black uprisings terrified southerners–and many northerners–and southern states were tightening their slave codes to curb black mobility. Some required blacks to carry special passes for travel; others banned all travel by blacks except to church meetings. Ten states were considering or had proposed changes in their state constitutions to ban voluntary emancipation of slaves by slaveholders.

Most House members responded to John Quincy's petitions for abolition with such hostility that he feared for the very future of the nation. He had entered Congress convinced "that this federative Union was to last for ages," but after his presentation, "I now disbelieve its duration for twenty years and doubt its continuance for five."[15]

In his self-appointed role as representative of the entire nation, John Quincy was determined to fulfill his obligation to his huge constituency by attending every session of Congress--from its first day on December 5, 1831 to its last, in March 1833–regardless of the weather or his own health.

He threw his mind and soul into his new work, studying rules and proceedings of previous Congresses, reviewing his law texts and the language of laws. His work brought new joy into his life–and misery into his wife Louisa's. Unlike his presidency, John Quincy's role as a Congressman did not generate the need to entertain at home, thus leaving Louisa with so little to do she took up fishing–and poetry writing. Even when John Quincy returned home, his mind, his heart, his soul remained in Congress. The only joy in her life came from caring for her two granddaughters.

As much as, and even more, than anything he had ever done in his life, John Quincy's work in Congress seemed to him the ultimate patriotic service he could perform for his country. "The forms and proceedings of the House," he exulted, were "a very striking exemplification of the magnificent grandeur of this nation and the sublime principles upon which our government is founded.

> "The colossal emblem of the Union over the Speaker's chair, the historic muse at the clock, the echoing pillars of the hall...the resolutions and amendments between the members and the chair, the calls of ayes and noes, with the different intonations...from the different voices, the gobbling manner of the clerk in reading over the names, the tone of the Speaker in announcing the vote, and the varied shades of pleasure and pain in the countenances of the members

on hearing it, would form a
fine subject for a descriptive
poem."[16]

It was not long before John Quincy

realized that Congress had not transduced his

petitions for abolition into legislative proposals;

although he kept presenting them, he knew he

would need his committee's support to produce

actual bills for enactment into laws.

He soon mastered all the intricacies of

American economics and manufacturing–especially

cotton and woolen goods manufacturing--and he

discovered the intricate ties between manufacturing

and a broad range of other issues, including foreign

affairs, tariffs and slavery. He now knew the way to

broaden the scope of his committee proceedings,

using the most obvious issue first–tariffs.

For a while, high tariffs on imported English

cotton goods had protected small New England

manufacturers against competition from British imports, but the tariffs that protected New England mills against British competition hurt southern cotton growers, who shipped more of their crop to British cotton mills than to New England. Southern planters demanded an end to the tariffs, and South Carolina's Governor called a special Nullification Convention in November 1832, which declared federal tariff laws null and void in South Carolin and threatened to secede from the Union if federal officials tried using force to collect tariffs.

A week later, the South Carolina legislature authorized raising a military force and appropriated funds for arms. Civil war seemed imminent.

The state's declaration and mobilization shocked the nation and left even President Jackson, a champion of states' rights, aghast. "The nation will be preserved," he declared angrily. "Perpetuity is stamped upon the Constitution by the blood of our fathers. Nullification therefore means insurrection and war, and the other states have a right to put it down."[17]

South Carolinians responded with huge demonstrations in Charleston. South Carolina Senator Robert Hayne resigned from the Senate to become governor of his state and lead the fight for nullification. Vice president Calhoun resigned as vice president, and rumors swept through Charleston that he intended returning to become first president of a Southern Confederacy.

On December 5, 1832, Jackson overwhelmed John Quincy's former secretary of state Henry Clay in the presidential election, with New York's Martin Van Buren winning the vice presidency. Five days later, President Jackson issued a presidential proclamation declaring "the power to annul a law of the United States, assumed by one state, incompatible with the existence of the Union" and warning of "dreadful consequence" for the "instigators" of the South Carolina Nullification Act.

"Disunion...is treason," he told the people of South Carolina. "On your unhappy heads will inevitably fall all raw evils of the conflict you force upon the government of your country."[18]

The summer recess postponed further Congressional debate over nullification until fall, and during that time, Harvard University voted to grant President Jackson an honorary degree. Although firmly on Jackson's side in the battle against nullification, John Quincy refused to attend the ceremonies honoring the President.

"As myself an affectionate child of our Alma Mater," he explained, "I would not be present to witness her disgrace in presenting her highest literary honors upon a barbarian who could not write a sentence of grammar and hardly could spell his own name."[19]

Although the summer began disagreeably, it ended in joy with the birth of his first grandson. His son and daughter-in-law named the baby John Quincy Adams II and ensured the preservation of the legendary Adams name in the United States for at least another generation. "There is no passion more deeply seated in my bosom," John Quincy exulted, "than the longing for posterity worthily to support my own and my father's name.... There is now one son of the next generation."[20]

John Quincy returned to Congress refreshed and ready to battle nullification, even if it meant strengthening ties to President Jackson. On January 16, 1833, with civil war threatening, Jackson asked

Congress to grant him authority to use military force if necessary to crush the nullifiers and enforce revenue and tariff collection laws. With John Quincy voting in favor, Congress complied. Jackson signed the Force Bill into law in March 2 and frightened South Carolina's legislature into rescinding its Nullification Act.

In December 1835, President Jackson sent Congress a curious and unexpected message: an Englishman, James Smithson, had left a bequest of about $500,000 to the United States "to found at Washington, under the name of the Smithsonian Institution, an Establishment for the increase and diffusion of knowledge among men."[21] Son of the first Duke of Northumberland, Smithson had, ironically, been half brother of General Hugh Lord Percy, the British commander at the Battle of Lexington in 1775. Although both houses of

Congress licked their collective chops at the possibilities for personal profits, the House acceded to John Quincy's fierce interest in science and named him chairman of the committee to determine how to disburse the money.

Besieged by schools and colleges for shares of the money, John Quincy ruled out disbursement of any of the principal, reserving it entirely to the government and limiting spending to interest generated by the principal. He intended combining George Washington's vision of creating "institutions for the general diffusion of knowledge" with his own vision of national astronomical observatories–the "lighthouses in the sky" that his political opponents had ridiculed when he was President. He called "the link between earth and heaven...the means of acquiring knowledge...therefore the greatest benefit that can be conferred upon mankind."[22] He was now prepared to fight his opponents in ways that eluded him when he was President.

South Carolina Senator John Calhoun, the former vice president, assailed John Quincy's proposal as federal government intrusion in an area the tenth amendment reserved for the states. He pointed out correctly that the Constitutional Convention had twice rejected efforts to give the government powers to establish a national university.

John Quincy countered, however, insisting there were no constitutional restrictions on establishing research institutions–nor did the framers restrict the national government from establishing any kinds of institutions in the District of Columbia. John Quincy won the day, with both houses deferring to his constitutional scholarship and approving his bill to establish the Smithsonian Institution as a public institution that remains in the hands of the American people to this day.

Despite President Jackson's proclamation that nullification was tantamount to treason, nullification fervor continued spreading in the South, and northerners responded with stepped up demands for abolition. Peering into the future, John Quincy warned that "a dissolution of the Union for the cause of slavery would be followed by...a war between the two severed portions of the Union. It seems to me that its result must be the extirpation of slavery from this whole continent and desolating as this course of events...must be, so glorious would be its final issue, that, as God shall judge me, I dare not say that it is not to be desired."[23]

As petitions demanding an end to slavery increased, he found abolitionists as prepared as slavery proponents to dissolve the Union to further their cause. For several years, therefore, beginning with the debate over the Missouri Compromise, he had argued that the Constitution failed to give Congress any powers to interfere with slavery in any state or territory in which it already existed. It could prevent its establishment in states and territories where it did not exist, but could not abolish it where it already did exist. Abolitionists countered, however, arguing that Congress could at least eliminate slavery in the District of Columbia, where it had powers to legislate and govern, unrestricted by the Constitution.

To end the sharp divisions over abolition, one congressman proposed: that "all petitions, memorials, propositions, or papers, relating in any way, or to any extent whatsoever, to the subject of slavery or the abolition of slavery shall without being either printed or referred, be laid on the table, and that no further action whatever shall be had thereon."[24]

The resolution, however, stepped beyond the abolition issue by clearly abridging free speech, and John Quincy all but exploded with rage, shooting to his feet for recognition. Speaker James K. Polk, a Tennessee slaveholder, ignored him and recognized only southern congressmen. John Quincy howled for recognition, but Polk looked the other way and, after southerners had finished their presentations, Polk put the resolution to a vote. The House approved it 95 to 82 and the speaker shut off all further debate, preventing John Quincy from saying a word.

3. Speaker James K. Polk

4.

"Am I gagged or am I not," John Quincy

shouted in disbelief and inadvertently giving the

new rule its historic name–the Gag Rule.

Southerners tried shouting him down with cries of

"Order!...Order!!" The Speaker called out over the

din, "The motion is not debatable," and when John

Quincy appealed to the House to overrule the

Speaker, it sustained the Speaker 109 to 89. When

the clerk called the Adams name, he stood: "If the

House will allow me five minutes in time..."

It did not. The House had silence his voice. Of his efforts in the House he concluded, "Never in my life have I taken in public controversies a part more suicidal to my own popularity."[25]

The Gag Rule infuriated Americans across the North and parts of the West as much as it did John Quincy, however, and hundreds of thousands of petitioners rallied to his side, arguing that if the House could gag the reading of petitions against slavery, it could gag petitions against or for anything. Women's rights groups joined the protests and added their own petitions to the flood already inundating Congress. When Maryland's Benjamin Chew Howard objected to the "unseemliness" of women presenting a petition, John Quincy sharpened his tongue and leaped for the rhetorical kill:

"Why, does it follow," he boomed, "that women are fitted for nothing but the cares of domestic life, for bearing children and cooking the food of a family, devoting all their time to the domestic circle–to promoting the immediate personal comfort of their husbands, brothers, and sons?" Louisa had apparently taught her husband to alter his thinking if not his ways.

"The mere departure of woman from the duties of the domestic circle, far from being a reproach to her, is a virtue of the highest order, when it is done from purity of motive, by appropriate means, and the purpose of good." He went on to read a petition opposing slavery from women in his constituency of Plymouth, Massachusetts:

"Is this discreditable?" he asked, before thundering his oft-repeated conviction: "I do believe slavery to be a sin before the sight of God."[26]

Recognized by then as an authority on parliamentary rules, John Quincy kept finding ways around the Gag Rule, at one point asking for recognition to read the prayers of a group of Massachusetts women. When a House member objected, John Quincy responded by explaining that the women were not petitioning but simply praying for "the greatest improvement that can possibly be effected in the condition of the human race–the abolition of slavery."[27]

The House exploded in collective anger at his flagrant violation of the ban on reading petitions against slavery and even uttering the word "slavery" in congressional debates. John Quincy smiled wryly, reiterating that he had not read a *petition* containing the word "slavery" [which he repeated], but a *prayer* of women, who, like the members' own mothers, were offended by "the sinfulness of slavery [again, the forbidden word!] and keenly aggrieved by its existence in a part of our country which..."

Choking in anger by then, South Carolina's Pinckney interrupted to charge John Quincy with reading a petition. "Point of order!" Pinckney bellowed.

"...keenly aggrieved by its existence in a part of the country over which Congress possesses exclusive jurisdiction in all cases whatever..."

"Order! Order!"

"...do most earnestly petition your honorable body..."

"Mr. Speaker! I rise on a point order!"

"...immediately to abolish slavery in the District of Columbia..."

"Mr. Speaker! A call to order!"

"Order! Order!"

"Take your seat!" the Speaker ordered John Quincy.

"...and..." John Quincy began to sit, accelerating his words as he did, "...to-declare-every-human-being-free-who-sets-foot-upon-its-soil."[28]

Increasingly stifled by the Gag Rule and its proponents, John Quincy finally ran out of parliamentary maneuvers and resorted to rhetorical trickery to confuse, embarrass, and, essentially, emasculate his political enemies.

Early in February, he presented two petitions, one from nine unnamed women and the other from actual slaves. As he knew they would, the southerners erupted in collective fury, with one

of them resolving that "infamous women...[and]

slaves do not possess the right of petition secured to

the people of the United States by the Constitution."

The same congressman resolved, as well, that any

member who presents a petition from slaves should

be considered "unfriendly to the Union," and his

third resolution–its content almost comical--cited

"the Hon. John Q. Adams" as having "disclaimed

all design of doing anything disrespectful to this

House." In effect, it accepted an apology from John

Quincy that he had never offered.

To prolong the charade, John Quincy asked

"for an opportunity for a full hearing in my

defense." He insisted he had never apologized and

resented the accusation of having done so. After the

laughter subsided, even Gag Rule sponsors relented,

recognizing that refusal to hear one of their own

colleagues might prevent each of them from
defending themselves in the future.

Focusing on the constitutional right of
petition rather than abolition, John Quincy asked,
"Will you put the right of petitioning, of craving for
help and mercy and protection on the footing of
political privileges?... No despot of any age or clime
has ever denied this humble privilege to the poorest
or meanest of human creatures.... That would be a
sad day, Sir...when a vote should pass this House
that would not receive a petition from slaves....
When the principle is once begun of limiting the
right of petition, where would it stop?"

John Quincy then accused the sponsor of the
resolutions of having accused the nine unnamed
women of prostitution

"I did not say they were prostitutes," the congressman protested in his southern drawl. "I have not said I know those women!"

"I am glad to hear the honorable gentleman disclaim any knowledge of them," John Quincy smirked, "for I had been going to ask, if they were infamous women, who it was that had made them infamous. Not their color, I believe, but their masters! I have heard it said in proof of that fact...that in the South there existed great resemblances between the progeny of the colored people and the white men who claim possession of them. Thus, perhaps the charge of infamous might be retorted on those who made it, as reflecting on themselves."

As southerners exploded with rage, "Old Man Eloquent," as the press now called John Quincy, could shout *touché*. It was a rhetorical triumph like no other in Congressional history at the time. Even the *Register of Debates* saw fit to note the response to John Quincy's words: "Great agitation in the House."[29]

Although the House voted down resolutions to censure John Quincy, it nonetheless voted to deprive slaves of the right to petition, thus eroding the sanctity of the Constitution and depriving most African-Americans of the privileges and protections of the Bill of Rights.

"Vengeance is mine, say the South!"warned a printed sheet someone slipped under John Quincy's door. Beneath a drawing of a whip were the words, "Flog and Spare Not!" Another letter addressed him as "Sir," but warned that "your conduct...is such as to draw upon you the indignation of the South.... The rod is cut that will make your old hide smart for your insidious attempt on southern rights.... If ever you dare to vindicate abolition again you will be lynched...drawing you from your seat in the House by force. So be on your guard."[30]

Thousands of northerners, however, wrote to support him, calling him the "Sage of Quincy," and urging him to "fear not southern insolence...we will defend and sustain you."[31]

The death threats terrified Louisa, who with John Quincy to retreat from his war with what he called the "slave-ocracy." She could do nothing to dissuade him. At 69, he was on fire, breathing the flames of freedom his father had lit and that he believed he had to maintain. As they approached their fortieth wedding anniversary, it was Louisa, not John Quincy, who turned to poetry and prayer for solace:

Grant, grant! O God a helping hand
And save us when we call;
Protect us 'gainst the murderer's hand;
Support us lest we fall.[32]

"I walk on the edge of a precipice in every step I take," John Quincy admitted, but, defying age, aching joints and the deterioration of his body, he found renewed strength in battle. He had never been to war, had always personified the perfect diplomat, but he now seemed fearless, felt fearless-- a knight charging into battle.

He pursued his daily routine of walking vigorously–defiantly–to and from his house and the Capitol–and swimming the Potomac nude. Occasionally, he misjudged his physical strength and agility and tripped and fell, suffering cuts and bruises and even dislocating his shoulder once–but he never missed a session of Congress. He believed the future of the nation was at stake, and he returned day after day to fight his war against the

"slaveocracy." And Quincy voters sent him back to

Congress again and again. Louisa fretted about his

health and safety, but she had lost all influence over

him and could do nothing to restrain him. He was

unstoppable–a meteor spiraling out of control in the

political firmament.

Humiliated by John Quincy's rhetorical

tactics, southerners began to shout "Expel him!"

whenever he spoke. "Expel him!" they repeated, as

he continued–sometimes prolonging his diatribes

against slavery for hours and, in one instance, for

parts of fifteen days.

John Quincy went beyond the halls of

Congress to the American people and became a

national presence, a force for justice and progress

that he had never been before–even as President of

the United States. Invited to speak throughout the

Northeast and parts of the West, he used traditional July 4 orations, along with eulogies on the deaths of Lafayette, then James Madison, to inveigh against slavery.

In 1736, Andrew Jackson decided to follow the precedent of earlier presidents and cede his office after two terms. His Democratic Party nominated vice president Van Buren of New York as their candidate to succeed Jackson.

Van Buren had used his presidency of the Senate to court anti-abolition sentiment in Congress and, in December, 1736, he scored an overwhelming victory over three other candidates, including Daniel Webster. John Quincy–by then towering over his House colleagues as champion of national interests--easily won re-election to the House without a party designation and without campaigning. Approaching seventy and feeling the effects of his age, he returned to Congress in 1737 determined to save his nation from destruction.

The House immediately reinstituted the Gag Rule, and John Quincy struck back, presenting more than two hundred petitions remonstrating against the Gag Rule as a violation of the Constitution, the rights of his constituents, "'and of my right of freedom of speech as a member of this House.'" The House responded with what he described as "war whoops of 'Order!'"[33]

Day after day, the struggle continued. During the 1837-1838 session alone, the American Antislavery Society sent the House 130,200 petitions, with untold thousands of names, to abolish slavery in the District of Columbia, 32,000 petitions to abolish the Gag Rule, 21,200 to forbid slavery in U.S. territories, 22,160 against admitting any new slave states, and 23,160 to abolish the slave trade between states.[34] Whenever John Quincy tried to comment on a resolution, the Speaker interrupted: "The gentleman from Massachusetts," he shouted, "must answer aye or no and nothing else! Order!"

"I refuse to answer," John Quincy fired back, "because I consider all proceedings of the House..." Again, the Speaker interrupted him, with shouts of "Order! Order!"

John Quincy slumped into his seat in response, but his voice persisted, "...a direct violation of the Constitution!"[35]

Around him came the cries, "Expel Him! Expel him!" from southerners, whose numbers grew ever greater with the growth of the slave population that could not vote. The increase in the number of slaves had increased the number of southern members of the House by 35 percent--enough to expel John Quincy, and they now prepared to do just that.

Chapter 4

Freedom Is the Prize

Washington's oppressive summer heat forced Congress to recess before proceeding against John Quincy Adams in 1839, and he was able to return home with Louisa to the cool breezes of Quincy Bay. When Congress reconvened in December, elections had divided the House evenly, and disorder attended every effort to establish committee memberships.

Deadlocked and facing legislative paralysis, Congress turned to the only man every member trusted, regardless of what they felt about his politics or him personally–and some genuinely hated him. But John Quincy Adams was the man who represented the whole nation, and, above all else, they knew John Quincy Adams to be that rarest of colleagues: an honest man and patriot.

Astonished by the sudden–and near-universal–embrace, John Quincy accepted the invitation and served as speaker *pro tem* long enough to work out committee memberships. When he succeeded to everyone's satisfaction and stepped down from his leadership role, they immediately turned on him again, reimposed the Gag Rule, and overrode his angry demands to repeal it.

Just then, however, his friend Ellis Gray Loring, a prominent Massachusetts attorney and outspoken opponent of slavery, drew John Quincy's attention away from the turmoil in Congress with some startling legal documents. In January 1840, a federal district court in New Haven, Connecticut, was about to hear the case of thirty-six Africans who been prisoners on the slave ship *Amistad* off the coast of Cuba. Led by a Congolese chief named

Cinque, they had broken their chains, killed the

captain and three crewmen, and overpowered the

white crew. Knowing nothing of navigation, they

ordered the white crew to sail them to Africa, and,

by day, the crew complied. At night, however,

crewmen reversed course and eventually sailed into

American waters, where an American frigate seized

it and took it to New London, Connecticut. Officials

there arrested the Africans and charged them with

piracy and murder, but a number of legal questions

complicated the case: Were the Africans *property*--

that is slaves--to be returned to their owners? Or

were they *people,* to be released on habeas corpus

and later tried for piracy and murder? And finally,

did the United States have jurisdiction? Or should

U.S. authorities release the prisoners to Spanish

authorities, to do with as they wished under Spanish law?

Picture No. 37. Killing of the captain of the *Amistad*

The district court pronounced the Africans to have been free men, whom slavers had kidnaped and transported to Cuba illegally–under Spanish as well as American law. It deemed the killings justified as legitimate acts of self-defense against their kidnappers and ordered the Africans turned over to the President of the United States for transport back to their native land at American government expense.

Having already alienated southerners by rejecting Texas annexation, President Van Buren was unwilling to further provoke his southern constituency and ordered the district attorney to appeal the lower court order to the circuit court. The circuit court upheld the district court and forced government prosecutors to take the case still higher to the U.S. Supreme Court. By then, however, abolitionists who had paid for the legal defense of the *Amistad* Africans ran out of funds, and all but two attorneys quit. Only Loring and Roger Sherman Baldwin, grandson of the revolutionary war hero, Roger Sherman, agreed to remain on the case *pro bono* without fees. They turned to John Quincy to join their appeal to the Supreme Court–also without a fee--and he agreed.

"Gracious heavens, my dear Sir," an outraged Virginian reacted to John Quincy's embrace of the Africans' defense. "Your mind is diseased on the subject of slavery. Pray what had you to do with the captured ship?... You are great in everything else, but here you show your weakness.

Your name will descend to the latest posterity with this blot on it: Mr, Adams loves the Negroes too much, *unconstitutionally*."[36]

Before the case reached the Supreme Court, 73-year-old John Quincy won re-election to the House by a two-to-one majority, while 68-year-old general William Henry Harrison, a hero of the Indian wars, defeated President Van Buren in the presidential election.

"The life I lead," John Quincy grumbled to his diary as he returned to Washington for double duty in Congress *and* the Supreme Court, "is trying to my constitution and cannot be long continued.

> My eyes are threatening to fail
> me. My hands tremble like an
> aspen leaf. My memory daily
> deserts me. My imagination is
> fallen into the sear and yellow
> leaf and my judgment sinking
> into dotage.... Should my life
> and health be spared to

perform this service...then will
be a proper time for me to
withdraw and take my last
leave of the public service.[37]

Before the *Amistad* appeal began, John

Quincy received a letter from one of his new

African clients, a member of an obscure tribe, the

Mendi. He had had no knowledge of English before

languishing in Connecticut jails for two years:

"Dear Friend Mr. Adams," the letter began:

I want to write a letter to you
because you love Mendi
people and you talk to the
Great Court. We want you to
ask the court what we have
done wrong. What for
Americans keep us in prison.
Some people say Mendi people
crazy dolts because we no talk
American language.
Americans no talk Mendi.
Americans crazy dolts?... Dear

friend Mr. Adams you have
children and friends you love
them you feel very sorry if
Mendi people come and take
all to Africa.... All we want is
make us free.[38]

On February 22, 1841, John Quincy walked

from his house to the Supreme Court, which sat in

the east wing of the Capitol beneath the Senate

floor. It was George Washington's birthday-- the

Founding Father John Quincy most revered after his

own father.

Uncompromising southern slaveholders

made up the majority of the nine judges, and John

Quincy knew them all. In the minority were Joseph

Story of Massachusetts, a former Harvard law

professor, and Chief Justice Roger B. Taney, a

Maryland slaveholder who would later free his

slaves. After the prosecution demanded that the

government return the *Amistad* Negroes to the

Spanish minister for restoration to their "owners,"

Roger Baldwin argued for the defense:

"The American people," he declared, "have

never imposed it as a duty upon the government of

the United States to become actors in an attempt to

reduce to slavery men found in a state of freedom

by giving extraterritorial force to a foreign slave

law."

The prosecuting attorney replied that slaves

"released from slavery by acts of aggression" do not

lose their status as the property of their rightful

owners "any more than a slave becomes free in

Pennsylvania who forcibly escapes from

Virginia."[39]

The next day, February 24, John Quincy

rose to address the court. "The courtroom was full,

but not crowded," he noted, "and there were not

many ladies. I had been deeply distressed and

agitated till the moment when I rose, and then my spirit did not sink within me. With grateful heart for aid from above...I spoke four hours and a half, with sufficient method and order to witness little flagging of attention by the judges."[40]

"Justice," he began, "as defined in the Institutes of Justinian nearly 2,000 years ago...is the constant and perpetual will to secure every one his own right....

> I appear here on behalf of thirty-six individuals, the life and liberty of every one of whom depend on the decision of this court.... Thirty-two or three have been charged with the crime of murder. Three or four of them are female children, incapable, in the judgment of our laws, of the crime of murder or piracy or, perhaps, of any other crime.... Yet they have all been held as close prisoners now for the period of eighteen long months.[41]

John Quincy told the justices of his distress

in prosecuting the government of his own nation

before the nation's highest court and, indeed,

"before the civilized world." But, he said, it was his

duty. "I must do it.

> The government is still in
> power...the lives and liberties
> of all my clients are in its
> hands.... The charge I make
> against the present executive
> administration is that in all
> their proceedings relating to
> these unfortunates, instead of
> that justice which they were
> bound not less than this
> honorable court itself to
> observe, they have substituted
> sympathy!--sympathy with one
> of the parties in this conflict
> and antipathy to the other.
> Sympathy with the white;
> antipathy to the black–and in
> proof of this charge, I adduce
> the admission and avowal of
> the secretary of state himself.[42]

John Quincy went on to read the letter from Secretary of State John Forsyth of Georgia to the Spanish minister in America, citing the owners of the *Amistad* "as 'the only parties aggrieved'–that all the right was on their side and all the wrong on the side of their surviving, self-emancipated victims.

"I ask your honors, was this justice?"[43]

Far from any "flagging of attention," the judges sat transfixed for more than four hours-- until other needs forced them to adjourn until the next day. That night, however, one of the justices died, and Chief Justice Taney postponed resumption of John Quincy's argument for a week.

The Court reconvened on March 1, with John Quincy summarizing his previous argument, then standing for three more hours, reiterating the argument that the *Amistad* Negroes had been free men, seized against their will on their native soil, kidnaped onto a ship, where they defended themselves and, in doing so, killed their kidnappers.

"What would have been the tenure by which every human being in this Union, man, woman, and child, would have held the blessing of freedom? Would it have been by the tenure of executive discretion, caprice, or tyranny...at the discretion of a foreign minister, would it not have disabled forever the effective power of *habeas corpus*?"

Then he came to the end of his presentation. Eschewing secular, legalistic appeals, "Old Man Eloquent" reached into his rhetorical reservoir for spiritual principles he believed he shared with every decent human being. In a moment that ensured his standing in the history of Congress and the Supreme Court, John Quincy Adams told the court that "more than thirty-seven years past, my name was entered and yet stands recorded on both the rolls as one of the attorneys and counselors of this court....

> I appear again to plead the cause of justice, and now of liberty and life, in behalf of many of my fellow men.... I stand before the same court, but not before the same judges.... As I cast my eyes along those seats of honor and of public trust, now occupied by you, they seek in vain for one of those honored and honorable persons whose indulgence listened then to my voice.[44]

After a dramatic pause, John Quincy turned his eyes toward the heavens, calling out the hallowed names of the Court's early justices--John Marshall, Bushrod Washington, and Thomas Todd of Virginia, William Cushing of Massachusetts and Samuel Chase of Maryland, William Johnson of South Carolina and Henry Livingston of New York. "Where are they?" he cried out, turning to focus on the faces of each of the justices. "Where?" he paused before lowering his voice to a near whisper.

Gone! Gone! All Gone! Gone from the
services which...they faithfully rendered
to their country.... I humbly hope, and
fondly trust, that they have gone to
receive the rewards of blessedness on
high. In taking leave of this bar and of
this honorable court, I can
only...petition heaven that every
member of it may...after a long and
illustrious career in this world, be
received at the portals of the next with
the approving sentence, "Well done,
good and faithful servant; enter thou
into the joy of the Lord."[45]

As tears flowed on spectator faces, the

prosecuting attorney shook his head in disbelief. He

had no idea what John Quincy's closing had to do

with the facts of the case, but members of the court

understood that by recalling the names of the

legendary justices who had helped establish the

nation's federal judiciary and, indeed, the nation

itself, John Quincy was asking them to abide by

standards higher than man's law. Accordingly, the

court voted unanimously to give its senior member,

Joseph Story, the honor of reading their

monumental decision on March 9:

> "There does not seem to us to be any
> ground for doubt that these Negroes
> ought to be free...."[46]

"Glorious!" Roger Sherman Baldwin roared

his congratulations to John Quincy. "Glorious not

only as a triumph of humanity and justice, but as a

vindication of our national character from reproach

and dishonor."[47]

John Quincy was equally elated. Calling his

courtroom triumph as one of the most notable

events in the family's illustrious history: "The

signature and seal of Saer de Quincy to the old

parchment [the Magna Carta]," John Quincy

bellowed, "were...almost my only support and

encouragement, under the pressure of a burden upon

my thought that I was to plead for more, much more than my own life."[48]

John Quincy's plea for the freedom of the *Amistad* captives marked more than six centuries that he and his forbears had led man's quest for freedom.

"Well done, good and faithful servant," he said to himself.

A flood of anonymous hate mail awaited John Quincy when he returned home. "Is your pride of abolition oratory not yet glutted?" asked a Virginian. "Are you to spend the remainder of your days endeavoring to produce a civil and servile war? Do you...wish to ruin your country because you failed in your election to the Presidency? May the lightening of heaven blast you...and direct you...to the lowest regions of Hell!"[49]

While John Quincy continued his daily walks and public swims unmolested, abolitionists paid the costs of sending the *Amistad* captives back to their homeland. After they left, a shipload of 135 slaves mutinied aboard the ship *Creole*, bound from Hampton Roads, Virginia, to New Orleans. After killing one of the owners, they directed the crew to sail to Nassau, where British authorities hanged those identified as murderers and freed the rest.

Although John Quincy had promised himself that if his life and health were spared to defend the men of the *Amistad,* he would "take my last leave of the public service," his Supreme Court triumph so elated him that he decided the time had not yet come to live up to his promise. "Fifty years of incessant active intercourse with the world," he now said to himself, "has made political movement to me as much a necessary of life as atmospheric air. This is the weakness of my nature, which I have intellect enough left to perceive, but not energy to control. And thus, while a remnant of physical power is left to me to write and speak, the world will retire from me before I retire from the world.[50]

A few days later, on April 4, 1841, President William Henry Harrison died of pneumonia after only a month in office. Vice president John Tyler, a fervent Virginia defender of states' rights and a champion of slavery, succeeded to the Presidency. With Tyler's warm approval, slaveholders in the House prepared to censure and expel John Quincy Adams.

Too elated by his Supreme Court triumph to notice the puerile antics of his Congressional enemies, John Quincy pursued his interests in the sciences, using his chairmanship of the committee on the Smithson bequest to promote establishment of astronautical observatories–his famous

"lighthouses of the sky."

He not only ignored the ridicule of

political foes, he gave his alma mater

Harvard $1,000 to help it build its own

observatory and loaned $13,000 of his own

money to Columbian College, the institution

"for the general diffusion of knowledge"

that George Washington had helped found

with a bequest in his will. It would grow to

become George Washington University.

4. President John Tyler

His constant glorification of the benefits of

astronomical observatories to expand man's

knowledge encouraged the Navy Department, the

University of North Carolina, Williams College,

Western Reserve College, Miami College (Ohio),

and the United State Military Academy to build observatories. Even Philadelphia's high schools built one–the Philadelphia High School Observatory, which opened a John Quincy Adams "Lighthouse of the Sky" to the citizens of the city. Ridiculing those who had scoffed at John Quincy's advocacy of such observatories, enlightened communities across the nation turned his vision into reality.

John Quincy's broad interest in science included insatiable curiosity about every new invention. As a boy, he had witnessed the first balloon flights in Paris and public demonstrations of Mesmer's then-new technique later known as hypnotism.

In 1839, another French inventor, Louis-Jacques-Mandé Daguerre, a scene-painter for the Paris opera, developed a process that used sunlight to make permanent pictures on metal plates. In 1843, American engraver Philip Haas opened a daguerreotype studio and John Quincy Adams asked him to take a photograph. Haas then produced the first surviving photograph of a living American President (see below).[51]

The *Amistad* case touched John Quincy in ways different from any previous experience, pushing him firmly into the abolitionist camp. Although they had failed to organize a full-fledged political party, northern abolitionists had nonetheless formed a powerful "Select Committee on Slavery" and rejoiced when John Quincy accepted their long-standing invitation to join.

5. Daguerreotype of John Quincy Adams

He joined, however, only on condition that they accept his leadership in matters concerning the House of Representatives, and the first thing he made them do was change their name to "Committee of Friends of the Right of Petition." The change cloaked their divisive abolitionist goal with the mantle of constitutional rights and broadened their appeal to defenders of the Bill of

Rights by calls to defend the rights of all Americans to petition and their rights to free speech.

When Congress convened in January 1842, John Quincy hoped his Supreme Court victory had covered him–and the Constitution--with enough laurels for the House to forget his corrupt bargain with Henry Clay and repeal the Gag Rule.

As he had at the beginning of every session since its imposition six years earlier, he opened the January 1842 session of Congress by assailing the Gag Rule as a clear violation of his own Constitutional rights to free speech and the rights of his constituents to petition government for redress of grievances. To these, he added the questionable constitutional right of uninterrupted free debate in Congress.

In renewing the Gag Rule, each session of Congress had extended its scope, so that instead of

simply banning the mention of the word "slavery,"
the rule now stated, "No petition, memorial,
resolution or other paper, praying for the abolition
of slavery in the District of Columbia, or any other
state or territory, or the slave trade between the
states and territories of the United States where it
exists shall be received by this House, or
entertained in any way whatsoever."

The increased strictures offended many
Congressmen unopposed to slavery in the South but
concerned only with its spread into other states and
territories. The new Gag Rule seemed too
restrictive. Far from the overwhelming majority that
had instituted the rule in1836, it passed by only four
votes in 1841, and John Quincy sensed victory near
as he honed his rhetorical weapons for 1842. He
picked what he knew "would set them in a blaze"–a
petition from "the citizens of Haverhill, in the

Commonwealth of Massachusetts...that you will immediately adopt measures peaceably to dissolve the Union of these States."[52]

As he knew it would, the parliamentary lynch mob from the South gathered about him, with cries of "Order!" "Stop him!" He raised his voice and continued above the din.

"Old Nestor," said an eye witness at the scene, "lifted up his voice like a trumpet, till slaveholding, slave trading, and slave breeding absolutely quailed and howled.... The old man breasted the storm and dealt blows upon the head of the monster. Scores...of slaveholders striving constantly to stop him by...screaming at the top of their voices, 'That is false!'...'I demand that you shut the mouth of that old harlequin.'"[53]

Kentucky Congressman Thomas Marshall, a nephew of the deceased Chief Justice John

Marshall, moved to censure John Quincy for having "committed high treason when he submitted a petition for the dissolution of the Union."

"Sir," John Quincy shot back, "what is high treason? The Constitution of the United States says what high treason is.... It is not for the gentleman from Kentucky, or his puny mind, to define what high treason is and confound it with what I have done." John Quincy then ordered the clerk to read the first paragraph of the Declaration of Independence." When the clerk hesitated, John Quincy repeated his demand, shouting, "The first paragraph!"

"When in the course of human events...

"...require that they should declare the causes which impel them to the separation..."

"Proceed!" John Quincy thundered. "Proceed! Down to 'right' and 'duty!'"

The clerk continued. "...it is their right, it is their duty, to throw off such government."

"Now, Sir, if there is a principle sacred on earth and established by the instrument just read, it is the right of the people to alter, to change, to destroy, the government if it becomes oppressive to them. There would be no such right existing if the people had not the power in pursuance of it to petition for it....

"I rest that petition on the Declaration of Independence!" John Quincy boomed.

When the House quieted down, he then challenged the right of the House to charge him with high treason, a crime for which, he said, "I could only be tried by a regular circuit court, by an impartial jury."[54]

Virginia's Henry Wise stood to contradict John Quincy, but made the tactical mistake of talking too much and digressing into a defense of "the principle of slavery" as "a leveling principle...friendly to equality. Break down slavery and you would with the same blow destroy the great democratic principle of equality among men." Wise had built a reputation as a staunch defender of slavery which he called "interwoven in our political existence...guaranteed by our Constitution...resulting from our system of government."[55]

After catcalls from northern congressman subsided, Wise got back on track, pretending to mourn John Quincy's having "outlived his fame.... To think of the veneration, the honor, the reverence with which he might have been loved and cherished.... I thank God that the gentleman, great as he was, neither has nor is likely to have sufficient influence to excite a spirit of disunion throughout the land.... The gentleman is politically dead."[56]

Far from politically dead, John Quincy found new life across the nation, as tens of thousands in the North and parts of the West rallied to his side. "When they talk about his old age and venerableness and nearness to the grave," Ralph Waldo Emerson reacted, "he is like one of those old cardinals who, as quick as he is chosen Pope, throws away his crutches and his crookedness and is as straight as a boy. He is an old roué, who cannot live on slops, but must have sulphuric acid in his tea."[57]

Gone and forgotten were any remnants of the "Corrupt Bargain" and his having stolen a presidential election. He had now wiped clean his slate.

When the time came for John Quincy's final defense against the attempt to quiet him, he challenged the southern parliamentary lynch mob, daring them to punish him for having presented the Haverhill petition.

"If they say that they will punish me, they must punish me. If they say that in grace and mercy they will spare my expulsion, I disdain and cast their mercy away.... I defy them. I have constituents to go to who will have something to say if this House expels me. Nor will it be long before gentlemen will see me here again."[58]

John Quincy then turned and pointed at Kentucky's Thomas Marshall, urging him to "go to some law school and learn a little of the rights of the citizens of these states and the members of this House."[59] John Quincy's public scolding sent Marshall scurrying back to Kentucky humiliated, with his intellectual tail between his legs, never again to return to national politics.

The debate continued for two weeks, with John Quincy's eloquence stirring the nation to petition Congress. Day after day, he held the floor, as petitions flew through the door protesting congressional attempts to censure him.

On February 7, he tried holding back a smile as he announced he would need another week to complete his defense, to which a member of the Virginia delegation moved to table the censure motion and end the matter.

When the House agreed, John Quincy responded by presenting 200 more petitions and addressing the House with one of the most momentous speeches he would ever deliver. Indeed, his words would later serve as the constitutional basis for Abraham Lincoln's Emancipation Proclamation.

"Under this state of things," he spoke, staring at the southerners, "so far from its being true that the states where slavery exists have the exclusive management of the subject, not only the President of the United States but the commander of the army has power to order the universal emancipation of the slaves."[60]

Years later, a southern defender of slavery would characterize John Quincy as the "acutest, astutest, archest enemy of southern slavery that ever existed...and his prophecies have been fulfilled...far faster and more fearfully...than ever he anticipated."[61]

John Quincy's triumph in the House provoked the usual hate mail, but the number of his supporters swelled across the nation, with one

Pennsylvanian writing, "You are honored, old man–

the hearts of a hundred thousand Pennsylvanians are

with you." Another called him "the only public man

in the land who possesses the union of courage with

virtue."

Poet John Greenleaf Whittier prayed, "God

bless thee, and preserve thee."[62] Even those who

had opposed the aggressive tactics of abolitionists

now wrote, "I am no abolitionist, yet I am in favor

of the emancipation of the colored race."[63]

His popularity exceeded that of the

President, and, had he defended his beliefs as

aggressively when he was President, he would

certainly never have suffered the humiliation of

defeat in his run for reelection. Few Americans

knew or understood him as President; almost every

American now knew and understood him–indeed,

revered him--after his battle in Congress–and

millions now listened to every word of the Sage of Quincy.

Hundreds lined up to see him, to hear his words, to try to talk to him as he walked about Washington, striding to and from the Capitol each day. Luminaries from all parts of the United States, Britain and Europe called at his home. Charles Dickens and his wife stopped for lunch and Dickens asked for John Quincy's autograph before leaving. John Quincy had emerged as one of the most celebrated and beloved personages in the western world.

In 1843, his son Charles Francis Adams, by then a member of the Massachusetts state legislature, introduced a resolution calling for a constitutional amendment abolishing the right of slave states to count five slaves as equal to three white men in determining representation in the

House of Representatives.

With deep pride, John Quincy, in turn,

introduced his son's amendment in the House--

which ignored it. After he won re-election in 1844,

however, the House could not ignore his resolution

abolishing the Gag Rule. Indeed, it passed it

immediately, 105-80, ending the great battle he had

fought for freedom of debate in Congress, freedom

of speech generally, and the right of citizens to

petition their government. It was the first victory the

North would win against the South and the

slaveocracy.

"Blessed, ever blessed be the name of God,"

John Quincy exulted afterwards.[64]

Riding his wave of popularity, he set off to

promote national interest in science and education

by accepting an invitation to speak at ceremonies

laying the cornerstone of the Cincinnati Astronomical Society's observatory. It was an arduous trip for an old man, but one with opportunities to promote science education–especially his "lighthouses of the sky"--across a broad territory.

He had no sooner received his invitation to speak in Cincinnati when another invitation arrived–this one to attend the long anticipated completion of the Bunker Hill monument, commemorating the battle he had witnessed as an eight-year-old with his mother in 1775. When, however, he learned that President John Tyler "and his cabinet of slave-drivers" would also attend, he refused. "How," he asked, "could I have witnessed this without an unbecoming burst of indignation or of laughter? John Tyler is a slave-monger....

With the association of the thundering
cannon, which I heard, and the smoke
of burning Charlestown, which I saw on
that awful day, combined with this
pyramid of Quincy granite and John
Tyler's nose, with a shadow
outstretching that of the monumental
column, I stayed at home and visited
my seedling trees and heard the
cannonades, rather than watch the
President at dinner in Faneuil Hall swill
like swine and grunt about the rights of
man.[65]

In November 1846, John Quincy suffered a

stroke while visiting his son Charles Francis in

Boston. Left speechless and confused, his right side

paralyzed, he seemed close to death; his doctors

gave his wife little hope for her husband's recovery.

As she kept vigil in his room each day, however, he

gradually recovered his speech, then his mind and

memory, and, by early December, he laughed off

his illness, snapping at his friends that he had

suffered only vertigo. But when he tried to stand

and walk, he fell; he could no longer support himself.

By Christmas, however, he was talking about returning to Congress and, on New Year's day, he set out for a ride in his carriage. A month later, on Sunday, February 7, sheer will power held him upright as he walked from his son's house to both morning and afternoon church services to take communion. The following morning he walked slowly, but magisterially onto the floor of the House and, as he took his seat, the members rose as one–North, South, East, and West–to cheer him. Among those celebrating his return was a tall, lanky, unkempt freshman congressman from Springfield, Illinois–Abraham Lincoln. During his short tenure in the House, Lincoln would prove one of John Quincy's strongest supporters–not just of abolition, but of Adams's proposals for federal initiatives in highway and canal construction and other forms of national expansion.

Picture No. 42. Congressman Abraham Lincoln

After Congress recessed in 1847, John Quincy insisted on returning to Quincy for the summer. Friends and relatives staged a gala eightieth birthday party for him on July 11, and, two weeks later, they feted John Quincy's and Louisa's golden wedding anniversary. John Quincy overwhelmed Louisa by giving her a beautiful bracelet that his son Charles Francis had purchased for him.

On November 1he returned to Washington, but the trip exhausted him–left him palsied, his entire body shaking. Too weak to speak audibly or to write, he walked unsteadily; he was nearly blind. He nonetheless insisted on taking his seat at the opening of the House on December 6, and Louisa conceded, "The House is his only remedy."[66]

Although he gave up all but one of his committee obligations and rode instead of walking to the House. He appeared for every roll call every day thereafter, and his face, if not his body, came to life when he heard a resolution supporting a Spanish government demand that the United States pay the *Amistad*'s owners $50,000 for the loss of their ship and its "cargo," which the Spanish minister characterized as a band of assassins.

On February 21, when the clerk read a resolution and called his name–his was third on the alphabetical roll–he tried to stand, his right hand gripping his desk as he rose. Then he slumped to his left–fortunately, into the arms of a fellow Congressman who had been watching him.

"Mr Adams is dying," cried a Congressman nearby. "Mr. Adams is dying," the words passed from member to member. Other members left and found a couch that they brought onto the House floor and helped their stricken colleague stretch out. Someone thought to ask for a formal adjournment. Both the Senate and Supreme Court followed suit when they learned of John Quincy's collapse. A group of Congressmen carried the sofa and its occupant into the rotunda to give John Quincy more air, but eventually moved it into the Speaker's office, where he revived enough to thank those around him and ask for Henry Clay, who arrived weeping. He clasped his old President's hand, unable to say a word before he finally left, unconsolable.

"This is the end of earth, but I am composed," John Quincy whispered, and lapsed into a coma. Eighty-year-old John Quincy lay in a coma

for the next two days, and, at 7:20 p.m., on

February 23, 1848, he died in the Capitol he adored.

Picture No. 43. Death of John Quincy Adams

The nation mourned as it had not since the

deaths of Washington and Franklin. John Quincy

lay in state in a committee room in Congress for

two days after his death; thousands filed by silently,

often not knowing why exactly, but somehow

realizing they had lost a champion of their rights–a

representative of no single constituency, state or

region, but of all Americans and of the whole

nation. He was an aristocrat of an earlier generation,

raised in an age of deference, who spoke a rich

language that ordinary people could seldom fathom,

but, in the end, they sensed that whatever he was

saying was for their own good and meant to protect

their rights   A single cannon blast awakened

Washington on Saturday morning, February 25;

another boom shook the city a minute later and

every minute until noon. Again, the multitude

reappeared, filling the streets like a great river

flowing to the Capitol. At 11:50, the bell on Capitol

Hill began to toll, and the President of the United

States led the justices of the Supreme Court, high

ranking members of the military, the diplomatic

corps, and members of the Senate into the House

chamber. John Quincy lay in a silver-framed coffin

on an elevated platform in front of the rostrum, his

eloquence resounding across the silent chamber:

> My cause is the cause of my country
> and of human liberty...the fulfillment of
> prophesies that the day shall come when
> slavery and war shall be banished from
> the face of the earth.[67]

With the President seated at the Speaker's right, the vice president at his left, and the portraits of Washington and Lafayette looking down on them all, the chaplain of the House prayed and set off what John Quincy's son Charles Francis Adams called "as great a pageant as was ever conducted in the United States." Choirs sang to the gods and orators lifted their voices to men, repeating the appeal for John Quincy's precious "Union."

When the assembly had intoned its final hymn, pall bearers carried the former President out of the Capitol to a silent multitude that stretched to the edge of the city. In the procession that followed, the speaker of the House led members of that body, the Senate, then President Polk, justices of the Supreme Court, the diplomatic corps, and an interminable line of military officials, state officials, craftsmen's organizations, college students, literary societies, firemen... It was endless–a collective outpouring of love and veneration the nation had rarely seen.

He lay in rest at the Congressional Cemetery for a week before the congressional committee of escort–a member from each state–came to take him aboard a train to Boston. Thousands lined the tracks northward to bow their heads as the train passed slowly, one car draped in black bearing John Quincy's coffin. The train stopped at various stations and crossings to allow citizens to climb aboard and say their goodbyes as they filed past him. Thousands awaited his arrival in Boston, where the congressional committee delivered the body of their colleague John Quincy Adams to Mayor Josiah Quincy, John Quincy's cousin and former president of Harvard, for transport to the family vault in Quincy.

A lifetime of friends and neighbors had gathered with his relatives and family to place John Quincy beside his father. As they laid John Quincy to rest, a small troop fired rifles in a last salute from nearby Penn's Hill, where John Quincy and his mother Abigail had watched the battle of Bunker's Hill and the beginning of the Revolution that spawned a new nation.

> *Day of my father's birth, I hail thee*
> *yet.*
> *What though his body moulders in*
> *the grave,*
> *Yet shall not Death th' immortal*
> *soul enslave;*
> *The sun is not extinct–his orb has*
> *set.*
> *And Where on earth's wide ball shall*
> *man be met,*
> *While time shall run, but from thy*
> *spirit brave*
> *Shall learn to grasp the boom his*
> *Maker gave,*

And spurn the terror of a tyrant's
threat?
Who but shall learn that freedom is
the prize
Man still is bound to rescue or
maintain;
That nature's God commands the
slave to rise,
And on the oppressor's head to
break his chain.
Roll, years of promise, rapidly roll
round,
Till not a slave shall on this earth be
found.
—John Quincy Adams, The White House, 1827.[68]

AFTERMATH

In the 230 years since the Constitution took effect, the Electoral College has elected five presidents who failed to win a majority of popular votes, and 214 "faithless electors" have disregarded voter preferences in 19 of 58 presidential elections. No "faithless electors" have ever been prosecuted.

Although Benjamin Franklin signed the Constitution, he was not enthusiastic: "I confess that I do not entirely approve this Constitution at present, but I am not sure I shall ever approve it."

Washington agreed, conceding imperfections, but citing Article V permitting future amendments to remedy defects.

The Constitutional Convention left each state free to decide how it would select its electors and whether or not electors would have to cast ballots according to voter preferences. To this day, no federal law prevents electors from disregarding preferences of those who appointed or elected them. In the 230 years since creation of the Electoral College, 214 "faithless electors" have disregarded voter preferences in 19 of 58 presidential elections. No "faithless electors" have ever been prosecuted.

The Electoral College elected five presidents who failed to win a majority of popular votes. The public punished four of the five by denying them second terms. Although the fifth—George W., Bush--won re-election narrowly, his two terms ended with a major economic recession and American involvement in two costly, indecisive wars in the Middle East. Presidential scholars ranked his administration as below average at 15th from the bottom among the more than 40 presidents in American history Donald Trump ranked the second worst president on the list; William Henry

Harrison 5th worst, John Tyler 7th, and Rutherford

B. Hayes 15th lowest. John Quincy Adams ranked

25th among the more than 40 presidents, and

Andrew Jackson ranked only a notch lower at 26th.

George Washington ranked 3rd best president

behind Abraham Lincoln (1) and Franklin D.

Roosevelt (2).

Washington, however, lived in a nation with

fewer than 50,000 eligible voters in a nation of 4

million people and 13 states. He did not--and could

not--envision his nation exploding into an empire

stretching from the Atlantic Ocean across one-

fourth of the planet's circumference, midway into

the Pacific. He did not--and could not--envision a

nation of approaching 400 million people in 50

states, each with conflicting and often irreconcilable

interests.

Despite perennial demands to replace the Electoral College with popular elections, every Congress has refused because reform would almost certainly reduce, if not eliminate the influence of underpopulated states.

Although twenty-nine states and the District of Columbia imposed laws against faithless electors, sanctions range from only token fines to mere nullification of their ballots. The U.S. Supreme Court has yet to rule on whether electors in the Electoral College must obey voters. If it fails to do so or if it rules to free electors of obligations to voters, it will open the Electoral College to foreign and domestic corruption that may end democracy in America as we know it. As things stand, state legislatures are corrupting the electoral process by enlarging or reducing the sizes of state voting districts to favor one political party or the other—squeezing large numbers of opposition

voters in one district and spreading friendly voters

into two, three, or more districts. Such legal

redistricting leaves that nation only a step away

from ensuring the corrupt bargain as the principal

method of determining future presidents of the

United States.

[Quotations from the Constitutional Convention in
Philadelphia in this article may be found in *The Records of the
Federal Convention of 1787*, Edited by Max Farrand (New
Haven, CT: Yale University Press, 4 vols., 1966), II:63-70
(Friday, July 20, 1787) and *Notes of Debates in the Federal
Convention of 1787 Reported by James Madison* (New York,
NY: W. W. Norton & Co., 1987), 331-336.]

Bibliography

Chase C. Mooney, *William H. Crawford, 1772-1834* (Lexington: University Press of Kentucky, 1974).
Paul C. Nagel, *John Quincy Adams: A Public Life, A Private Life* (Cambridge: Harvard University Press, 1997).

Allan Nevins, ed., *The Diary of John Quincy Adams, 1794-1845* (New York: Charles Scribner's Sons, 1951).

Lynn Hudson Parsons, *John Quincy Adams* (Lanham, MD: Rowman & Littlefield Publishers Inc., 1998).

"	*The Birth of Modern Politics: Andrew Jackson, John Quincy Adams and the Election of 1828* (New York: Oxford University Press, 2009).

Robert V. Remini, *John Quincy Adams* (New York: Henry Holt and Company, 2002).

Henry Clay: Statesman of the Union (New York: W. W. Norton, 1991).

The Life of Andrew Jackson (New York: Harper and Row, 1977-1984, 3 vols.).

Harlow Giles Unger, *John Quincy Adams* (Philadelphia: Da Capo Press, 2012).

Henry Clay, America's Greatest Statesman
(Philadelphia: Da Capo Press, 2015).

Manuscript Collections

Boston Atheneum

Bostonian Society

Boston Public Library

Houghton Library, Harvard University

Library of Congress, Washington, D.C.

Massachusetts Historical Society, Boston

The Adams Family Papers

*The Diaries of John Quincy Adams, A
Digital Collection* (51 vols., 14,000+ pages
online)

Adams Family Correspondence

Notes

[1] *The Papers of Henry Clay*, James F. Hopkins,
editor, The University Press of Kentucky, Lexington, KY,
1972, Volume 4, 1825, p. 11

[2] January 9, 1825, entry in John Quincy Adams,
Diary of John Quincy Adams, 2 vols., Cambridge, MA;
Belknap Press of Harvard University, 1981

[3] Reprinted from *Maryland Gazette*, 29 January 1788

4. Andrew Jackson to John Overton, February 14,
1825, Rimini, 155.

5. Rimini, 153.

6. *Diary*, February 28, 1829, MHS.

7. Ibid., September 24, 1829.

8. Wharton, 242-245.

9. *Diary*, November 7, 1830, MHS.

10. Morris, 130.

11. John Quincy Adams, *Life of James Monroe*, a
eulogy delivered in Boston, July 4, 1831, Koch and Peden,
373-379.

12. John Quincy Adams, *The Lives of James Madison and James Monroe, Fourth and Fifth Presidents of the United States* (Rochester, NY: Erastus Darrow, Publisher; Buffalo: Geo. H. Derby and Co., 1850), 288-289.

13. *Diary*, December 12, 1831.

14. Ibid.

15. Ibid., February 2, 1832.

16. Ibid., February 20, 1832.

17. Andrew Jackson to Joel Poinsett, November 29, 1832, in Rimini, 235.

18. J. D. Richardson, *Compilation of Messages and Papers of the President* (Washington, D.C., 1908, 20 vols.), II:1203-1217.

19. *Diary*, June 18, 1833, MHS.

20. *Memoirs,* 9:18.

21. *Smithsonian Miscellaneous Collections: Documents Relating to the Origins and History of the Smithsonian Institution*, William J. Rhees, ed. (Washington: Smithsonian Institution, 1880), 1-2.

22. Report of Mr. John Q. Adams from the Select Committee of the House of Representatives on the *Smithsonian Bequest*, in the House of Representatives, December 21, 1835, and published in the *National Intelligencer*, February 17, 1836.

23. *Diary*, November 29, 1820, MHS.

24. *Register of Debates*, XII, Pt. III, 3758-78, May 18-19, 1836.

25. *Diary*, March 18, 1835, MHS.

26. Bemis, *Union*, 369-370.

27. Ibid., 341.

28. *Register of Debates*, XIII, Pt. I, 1314-1339, January 8, 1837.

29. Ibid., XIII, Pt. II, 1586-1735.

30. "Dirk Hatteraik" to JQA, February 10, 1837, in AP MHS.

31. "Justice" to JQA, April 28, 1837, AP MHS.

32. Jack Shepherd, *The Adams Chronicles: Four Generations of Greatness* (Boston: Little, Brown and Company, 1975), 332.

33. *Diary*, December 21, 1837, MHS.

34. Statistics obtained from Bemis, *Union*, 340.

35. Ibid., December 14, 1838.

36. "A Virginian" to JQA, December 31, 1839. AP MHS

37. *Diary*, November 11, 1840, MHS.

38. Ka-le to JQA, January 4, 1841, AP MHS.

39. Bemis, *Union*, 407-408.

40. *Diary*, February 24, 1841, MHS.

41. *Argument of John Quincy Adams Before the Supreme Court of the United States...*, originally published by S.W. Benedict, 1841, http://www..historycentral.com/amistad/amistad.html

42. Ibid.

43. Ibid.

44. *Memoirs*, 10:436-437.

45. Ibid.

46. Bemis, *Union*, 410.

47. Roger S. Baldwin to JQA, March 12, 1841, AP MHS.

48. Ibid., JQA to CFA, April 14, 1841.

49. Ibid., Anonymous (from Dumfries, Va.) to JQA, June 15, 1841.

50. *Memoirs*, 10: 450-451, March 23, 1841.

51. By 1845, Plumbe had opened a chain of 25 studios and, working out of his Washington studio in that same year, he became the first photographer to make a portrait of a sitting president–James K. Polk. His other subjects included Dolley Madison, Daniel Webster, Martine Van Buren, and John James Audubon. Although photographers took portrait shots of Andrew Jackson, Martin Van Buren, William Henry Harrison, John Tyler and James K. Polk all had photo-portraits but John Quincy Adams, although out of office, was the earliest American President ever to be photographed.

52. *Memoirs*, 11:71.

53. Bemis, *Union*, citing Theodore Weld to Angelina G. Weld and Sarah Grimké, January 23, 1842, *Weld-Grimké Letters*, II, 899-1000.

54. *Memoirs*, 11:73-74.

55.*Register of Debates*, XI, Pt. II, 1399.

56. Bemis, *Union*, 432.

57. Ibid., 56.

58. Bemis, 434-435; *Congressional Globe*, XI, 208.

59. *Congressional Globe*, 168-208.

60. Allan Nevins, ed., *The Diary of John Quincy Adams, 1794-1845* (New York: Charles

Scribner's Sons, 1951), xxvii.

61. Barton H. Wise, *The Life of Henry Wise of Virginia, 1806-1876* (New York, 1899), 61-62, cited in Bemis, *Union*, 436-437.

62. Letters to JQA from Isaac Fisher (February 15, 1842), William Shinn (March 4, 1842), John Greenleaf Whittier (January 31, 1842), AP MHS.

63. T. H. Brower to JQA, February 8, 1842, AP MHS.

64. *Memoirs*, 12:116.

65. Ibid., 11, 383.

66. Louisa Catherine Adams to her niece Abigail Brooks Adams, December 9, 1847, reel 536,

AP MHS..

67. *Diary*, November 12, 1842, MHS.

68. *Memoirs*, 7:164, mistakenly published in his *Memoirs* as written on October 30, 1826. In his old age, JQA had slipped the undated poem at random between pages of his

diary bearing the 1826 date, and his son, Charles Francis, in

compiling his father's *Memoirs* for publication, assumed that

was the date on which his father had written it.